Shia Muslims

Shia Muslims

Our Identity, Our Vision, and the Way Forward

Sayyid M. B. Kashmiri

I.M.A.M.

IMAM MAHDI ASSOCIATION OF MARJAEYA

Imam Mahdi Association of Marjaeya, Dearborn, MI
48124, www.imam-us.org
© 2017, 2018. by Imam Mahdi Association of Marjaeya
All rights reserved. Published 2018.
Printed in the United States of America
ISBN-13: 978-0-9982544-9-4

Second Edition

Contents

Contents

Preface

In the name of God, the All-Beneficent, the All-Merciful

May blessings and peace be upon His prophet and the best of His creations, Muhammad and his pure and infallible progeny

The United States of America is characterized by traits that have guaranteed its progress and marked its excellence among other nations in recent history. One of the prominent features of the United States of America is its ability to embrace a diversity of cultures and a variety of schools of knowledge by attracting their leaders and followers from around the world.

There is no doubt that cultural and informational diversity is a requirement for progress and prosperity, and it has the potential to improve quality of life. The Almighty Creator of the world and humankind speaks of it as He says, "Among His signs is the creation of the heavens and the earth, and the difference of your languages and colors. There are indeed signs in that for those who know" (Quran 30: 22),[1] and "Were it not for God's repelling of the people by means of one another, the earth would surely have been corrupted; but God is gracious to the world's creatures" (Quran 2: 251).

Today, Muslims constitute a significant portion of the cultural and intellectual demographic of the United States. We have a presence in many fields and contribute to them at all levels; sometimes these contributions are minor, but at other times they are crucial and pivotal.

Thus, we American Muslims no longer see ourselves as isolated and marginalized. We have voiced our opinions and are increasingly being noticed in every stratum of society, particularly given immigration and a growing family structure that has produced second and third generations that value citizenship and coexistence. Indeed, the emergence of American Muslims in the public's awareness and our now seemingly permanent position there has been due to the global events of the last two decades. These include not only the tragedy of September 11, 2001, the wars on the terroristic Taliban in Afghanistan, and the dictatorial Baathist regime in Iraq, but also other events that have changed the course of history and altered the identity of many nations. Thus, in the same way that other groups have become integrated in the

United States after many decades of isolation and marginalization, Muslims in America are becoming mainstream.

Because of this trend, awareness of Muslim values is growing, and the American public is willing to learn about the details of our lives and the diversity of our denominations. In part due to the influence of the media, it has become normal for people to ask American Muslims which sect we belong to, either casually or out of curiosity. This contrasts with what happens in countries inflamed by sectarian strife where the same question often has a hidden agenda.

As such, we American Shia (Arabic: شيعة) Muslims, who have been encouraged by our leaders to integrate and coexist while simultaneously preserving our religious identity and noble traditions, have become the subject of inquiry by our fellow citizens with whom we share common patriotic concerns. Hence, we Shia Islamic leaders are increasingly invited to introduce Islam from the perspective of the progeny of the Prophet, and our continued presence in scholarly discussions, research forums, and academic conversations is being noticed. These contributions enrich knowledge and educate others about the culture of Shia Muslim American citizens who are full of giving and sacrifice for their country and for a safe life.

After receiving many requests about Shia Muslims from seminar attendees, I saw fit to write a booklet that is easy to understand for those interested in getting to know the principles and goals of Ithna Ashariyya (Arabic: إثنا عشرية "Twelver")[2] Shia Muslims in a clear and genuine way. I am hoping it will be a good introduction and a door to further investigation and learning. Today we live in an exceptional and complex time with vast information in global media where there is ample risk of getting lost and misinformed. Thus, this booklet intends to clarify misinformation and to fulfill the wishes of those who requested it. It is easy to hold and carry around, and I hope it is also easy to read and understand.

In writing it, I have relied on the doctrines, provisions, and reflections that prominent Shia Muslim scholars have abided by and been inspired by—the glorious Quran, the teachings of the infallibles, consensus,[3] and reason. I hope it is worthy and useful.

Finally, I would like to thank everyone who has contributed to preparing this booklet, whether by giving guidance, ideas, or thoughts. I would also like to thank my spouse, Haja Zeinab, who provided a calm environment, who was patient and agreeable, and who shouldered the extra responsibilities of our family and four children in addition to her other obligations and commitments so that I could have the opportunity to serve the religion and society. I present this effort to her along with its heavenly reward.

Sayyid M. B. Kashmiri
Fairfax, Virginia

Our Identity

The doctrine we believe in and the religious principles we adopt to draw a complete picture that will define our religious identity

Our Vision

Our outlook and motivations in life, which are based on the religious beliefs we hold

The Way Forward

The steps we need to take and the process we need to follow to achieve our goals based on our religious beliefs

Our Identity

Our Identity

Like all other groups, communities, and nations, Shia Muslims have a clear, precise, and genuine identity that is based on core pillars: monotheism, the hereafter, justice, prophethood, and leadership.

Monotheism (Tawhid, Arabic: التوحيد)

Monotheism is the common foundation and core principle that all Shia Muslims adhere to, irrespective of our subgroupings. Monotheism is the belief that

- there exists a God who is the cause of all causes, who is conceptually known as the Necessary Being;
- God is one and He is the only god: "He neither begat, nor was begotten, nor has He any equal" (Quran 112: 3–4);
- by proving the existence of God, the complete qualities of knowledge, power, justice, wisdom, sufficiency, and all other good qualities are proved to be manifest in Him. He is also deemed far above bad qualities such as injustice, unfairness, frivolity, and any other quality that implies deficiency and need. God is not an object

and is not confined by space and time dimensions. He is deemed far above anything human beings can conceive. "Nothing is like Him" (Quran 42: 11).

The Hereafter (Ma'ad, Arabic: المعاد)

Prominent scholars recognize that most religions agree on the inevitability of life after death and the Day of Resurrection. All prophets talked about the hereafter and life after death whenever they talked about monotheism. This belief was among the first they called people to accept. Thus, it is one of the pillars of Islam. Although the hereafter is mentioned in the Torah and the Bible, the Quran gives it more prominence than other divine books and repeatedly emphasizes it.

The hereafter is mentioned in the Quran using various names, such as the Day of Rising, the Day of Reckoning, the Last Day, the Day of Resurrection, the Day of Dispossession, the Day of Regret, and others. The reason for all this attention to the Day of Resurrection is that faith and piety cannot bear fruit without belief in the Day of Resurrection as the day of reward. Belief in the hereafter is considered a necessary religious belief. There are clear, rational, textual proofs of it, particularly in the Quran.

God, the Almighty, is pure righteousness, and His work is righteous and far from any evil or frivolity. Thus, creating humankind without the existence of an eternal life is frivolity, as God affirms when He says, "Did you suppose that We created you aimlessly, and that you will not be brought back to Us?" (Quran 23: 115).

In verses 78–79 of chapter 36, the Quran states, "He [man] draws comparisons for Us, and forgets his own creation. He [man] says, 'Who shall revive the bones when they have decayed?' Say, 'He will revive them who created them the first time, and He has knowledge of all creation.'" These serve as outright stipulations attesting to the existence of the hereafter and denouncing its disbelievers and deniers.

Divine justice prevents good-doers and wrong-doers from receiving the same reward. Many wrong-doers depart from this world without being held accountable for their wrongdoings, or they may get a light punishment that is disproportionate to their evil and crimes while the conditions of righteous believers in this world may be much worse than the conditions of the disobedient wrong-doer. Therefore, complete justice cannot be realized in this life because the deeds of both doers of good and doers of evil are intermingled and inseparable. Furthermore, the reward or punishment for some acts, whether good or evil, cannot be fulfilled in this life. Should the state of someone who sacrifices themselves to promote righteousness be the same as the state of someone who kills innocent people? Should the reward of the martyr be restricted to worldly death or should the reward be proportionate to the sacrifice (i.e., beyond this world)?

Thus, there should be another world where complete divine justice is realized with infinite giving and compensation. The Almighty says, "Shall We treat those who have faith and do righteous deeds like those who cause corruption on the earth? Shall We treat the Godwary like the vicious?" (Quran 38: 28). He also says, "To Him will be the return of you all—[that is] God's true promise. Indeed, He originates the creation, then He will bring it back that He may reward those who have faith and do righteous deeds with justice. As for the faithless, they shall have boiling water for drink, and a painful punishment because of what they used to defy" (Quran 10: 4).

The creation of a human in this world begins with a single sperm and ovum. It then progressively grows until God breathes His spirit into it. The Quran describes the creator of the universe as "the best of creators" for His creation of humankind is in "the best of forms." By dying, a human moves from this world to another world, and progresses toward an advanced level. The Quran points to this idea by saying, "Then We produced him as [yet] another creature. So, blessed is God, the best of creators. Then indeed you die after that. Then you will indeed be raised up on the Day of Resurrection" (Quran 23: 14–16).

Justice (Adl, Arabic: العدل)

Muslims unanimously accept that divine justice is the main attribute to which all other divine attributes trace back. The focus of this justice is to deem God, the Almighty and Immaculate, far above any kind of unjustness and unfairness because He is the "maintainer of justice." He, the Immaculate, says, "Indeed God does not wrong [anyone] [even to the extent of] an atom's weight" (Quran 4: 40), and "God bears witness that there is no god except Him—and [so do] the angels and those who possess knowledge— maintainer of justice" (Quran 3: 18).

In addition, reason itself asserts the necessity of divine justice. That is because justice is an attribute of perfection while injustice is an attribute of deficiency, and reason maintains that God has all the attributes of perfection and is far from any flaw or fault. Injustice happens because a perpetrator is ignorant of an act's hideousness, because they have a need to commit the act, or due to foolishness and recklessness. These are inconceivable about God because the proof for monotheism provides that He is all-knowing, all-sufficient, and all-wise, and so He cannot make any such mistakes.

This is the mainstream Muslim doctrine. However, some Muslims believe in the possibility of God committing some injustice because of their partiality toward some incorrect and feeble assumptions. They reason that the human brain is not capable of comprehending the goodness and ugliness of actions and that goodness and ugliness can be understood by divine revelation only. As a result, they say that there is no good or ill without God's decree and that what God has commanded is good and what He has forbidden is ill. So, these misguided Muslims believe that God decrees the ill (i.e., injustice) and causes it to happen even though He has forbidden it. On the other hand, mainstream Muslims, in particular Imami Shia scholars and those of the Mutazilah (Arabic: المعتزلة)[4] sect, assert that every human being can comprehend the goodness of justice and the hideousness of injustice just as they can comprehend the goodness of keeping promises and the hideousness of breaking them as well as the goodness of reciprocating favors and the hideousness of not doing so. The study of humanity's history testifies to this fact and confirms it, and no wise person would deny it. Thus, the Imami (Arabic: الإمامية "Twelver") and Mutazilah sects believe in the impossibility of divine injustice because injustice is itself hideous, and the hideous cannot be attributed to the all-wise Creator.

Although nothing happens without God's will, people have been given freedom of choice, which often can be the cause of evil. This delegation of choice from God to us places the blame of injustice on human beings and can never be attributed to God because it is we who make the conscious decision to commit indecent acts.

Realms of justice
Divine justice is manifest in three realms: creation, legislation, and recompense.

The realm of creation
In the realm of creation, we find that God has given every creature what it needs and what is suitable for it. At the time of creation, God did not neglect the

capabilities of any creature. The Quran says, "Our Lord is He who gave everything its creation and then guided it" (Quran 20: 50).

The realm of legislation

In the realm of legislation, we notice that God has guided humankind, who possesses the ability to grow and reach moral perfection, by sending prophets and legislating religious laws. Also, God did not burden human beings with what exceeds their capabilities. He, the Almighty, says, "God does not burden any human beyond its capacity" (Quran 2: 286). Therefore, God has distinguished those He chose to be prophets and their trustees by making them the only ones to set the example for human life on Earth. "They are the ones whom God has blessed from among the prophets of Adam's progeny, and from [the progeny] of those We carried with Noah, and from among the progeny of Abraham and Israel, and from among those We guided and chose" (Quran 19: 58). God gave only them the power to administer His laws, because administration without justice and impartiality, even for one instance, is injustice and partiality.

The realm of compensation

In the realm of compensation, we notice that God never treats the believer and the unbeliever or the benefactor and the harmful in the same way. He compensates each of them according to their deeds. Therefore, He does not punish a person who was not informed about His commands and instructions by means of prophets and messengers or a person who did not receive the full proof. God asserts, "We do not punish [any community] until We have sent [it] an apostle" (Quran 17: 15), and "We shall set up the scales of justice on the Day of Resurrection, and no soul will be wronged in the least" (Quran 21: 47).

Prophethood (Nubuwwah, Arabic: النبوّة)

God sends messengers and prophets because He is just. Their message has both temporal and spiritual benefits to human beings. The message is for the benefit of human beings and deters them from corruption. God sent messengers and prophets as bearers of good news and givers of warning, choosing them with care, and facilitating favorable conditions for them that suit the roles that He chose them to play.

They are supreme examples for humanity of knowledge, values, morals, giving, and sacrifice.

There were one hundred twenty-four thousand

prophets—the first being Adam, the father of humanity, followed by Noah, Abraham, Moses, Jesus, and, finally, Muhammad son of Abdullah (53 BH–11 AH, 570–632 CE).

The message

The 'message' refers to the religion of Islam, which is the seal of religions and the divine law in its final, integrated form. It manifests itself in the demeanor and tacit approval *sunnah* (Arabic: سُنَّة)[5] of the Prophet and his successors, in their instructions, and in the eternal miracle, the Quran. The Quran is the book that God revealed to His last prophet, Muhammad son of Abdullah.

The Quran says in some of its verses that it was revealed by two methods—full revelation and gradual revelation.

Full revelation

Full revelation is the descent of the Quran physically and spiritually as one integral truth into the heart of Muhammad son of Abdullah on the Night of Ordainment. "Indeed, We sent it down on the Night of Ordainment" (Quran 97: 1). And "Indeed We sent it down on a blessed night, and indeed We have been warning [mankind]" (Quran 44: 3).

Gradual revelation

Gradual revelation is the detailed textual descent of the Quran, verse by verse, during twenty-three years beginning with the first message when Archangel Gabriel descended to Prophet Muhammad in the cave of Hira, which is near Mecca, and ending with his departure from this world in Medina.

The Prophet had a complete comprehension of the message through full revelation. However, he only transmitted what God permitted and wanted him to transmit to people. God, the Immaculate, says, "Do not move your tongue with it to hasten it. Indeed, it is up to Us to put it together and to recite it. And when We have recited it, follow its recitation" (Quran 75: 16–18).

That is because of the ultimate goal that only God, the Almighty and Immaculate, knows: "We have sent the Quran in [discrete] parts so that you may read it to the people a little at a time, and We have sent it down piecemeal" (Quran 17: 106). Thus, the Quran was revealed according to the events and developments of the time.

It began with the first descent of Gabriel to the Prophet in the cave of Hira when he was forty years old carrying the first verses of the chapter of the Clinging Mass, and it ended with what was revealed to him before his departure from this world, which were the chapter of the Help[6] and the verse of perfecting the religion and completing the blessing,[7] which occurred after the farewell pilgrimage by the Ghadir Khumm[8] on the eighteenth day of the month of Dhu al-Hijjah[9] of the tenth year AH. Soon after, near the end of the month of Safar of the eleventh year AH, he departed this world.

God revealed the Quran to His final prophet through His favorite angel, Gabriel. God says in the Quran, "This is indeed [a Book] sent down by the Lord of all the worlds, brought down by the Trustworthy Spirit, upon your heart (so that you may be one of the warners" (Quran 26: 192–194).

Speaking through angels is one of many ways in which God speaks to His prophets. God says in the Quran, "It is not [possible] for any human that God should speak to him except through revelation or from behind a curtain, or send a messenger who reveals by His permission whatever He wishes. Indeed, He is all-exalted, all-wise" (Quran 42: 51), meaning either by direct inspiration, from beyond the physical world such as from behind a mountain or a tree, or through the angel Gabriel.

The Quran that was revealed to Prophet Muhammad is

what is, in book form, circulated among Muslims today. It is the same book with no addition or reduction. It contains 114 chapters, starting with the chapter of the Opening and ending with the chapter of Humans. It is the book referred to in the famous tradition (*hadith*) that is narrated by Hafs quoting Assim al-Kufi quoting Imam Ali son of Abu Talib quoting God's prophet, is circulated everywhere, and is accepted by the all Muslims. Anyone who claims otherwise is either mistaken or a deceitful slanderer.

Leadership (Imamate, Arabic: الإمامة)

Just as prophethood stems from God's justice because of people's need for bearers of good news, advisors, and leaders, leadership (imamate) also stems from God's justice for the same reason. The reason is that, while their message is eternal, prophets and messengers are limited in time by the number of years they stay in this world: "Say 'I am just a human being like you. It has been revealed to me'" (Quran 18: 110). Because Prophet Muhammad is the seal of the prophets and there is no prophet after him, divine wisdom has required the appointment of competent successors to succeed him. They complement his mission and manage the implementation of his message. They instruct people to do good and righteousness without corruption and perversity so that creation's divine goal of worshipping God and implementing His religion and law is achieved not only by individuals but by society. This fulfills divine justice on Earth and assures God's will of having a viceroy on it who has all the attributes that He has imbued and that originate from justice. God has guaranteed this and made choosing them one of His own prerogatives. God said in response to Prophet Abraham's wish, "And when his Lord tested Abraham with certain words and he fulfilled them, He said, 'I am making you the Imam of mankind.' Said he, 'And from among my descendants?' He said, 'My pledge does not extend to the unjust'" (Quran 2: 124). This is because genealogical relations do not guard one against being unjust, whether that unjustness is directed toward oneself, others, or even toward God's property.

Thus, it is required that the successor be chosen by God and be a high achiever in doing good. "That which We have revealed to you of the Book is the truth, confirming what was [revealed] before it. Indeed, God is all-aware, all-seeing about His servants. Then We made heirs to the Book those whom We chose from Our servants. Yet some of them are those who wrong themselves, and some of them are average, and some of them are those who take the lead in all the good works by God's will. That is the greatest grace [of God]!" (Quran 35: 31–32) and "Certainly We chose them knowingly above all the nations" (Quran 44: 32). Moreover, God, the Almighty and Immaculate, says, "God knows best where to place His apostleship" (Quran 6: 124). He placed it in prophets He chose and successors He selected. There is no place here for voting and consultation, because this is God's "affair" that He has not prescribed for anyone other than Himself. This contrasts with other trivial subjects such as people's everyday affairs that He left to them and said, "And their affairs are by counsel among themselves" (Quran 42: 38). The human "affairs" referred to in this verse are different from His "affair," which is related to divine leadership, prophecy, and its successorship and which is solely subject to His authority. The Prophet declared, in many instances and settings, something that thousands of narrators of hadith have transmitted (including the hadith of the Ghadir Khumm that was narrated by more than one hundred of the companions of the Prophet and was cited by numerous sources of various Islamic sects in addition to Shia sources): that the Prophet appointed Ali son of Abu Talib to be his successor. Ali was the first believer and the one whom Prophet Muhammad kept for himself to be his brother on the day of brotherhood between the Muhajirun[10] and Ansar.[11] He said to him, "I saved you for myself, and you are my brother, my trustee, and my successor after I leave, but you are not a prophet."

There is also the oft-repeated hadith of the Two Weighty Things, when the Prophet said, "I am leaving among you the two weighty things: the Book of God and my progeny, the members of my household. If you hold fast to them, you will not go astray." This hadith was narrated by dozens of narrators in various ways and is mentioned in all the prominent Islamic hadith collections in addition to Shia sources such as the *Al-kafi* collection, the *Jami ahadith al-Shia* collection, and hundreds of other sources. What has been propagated and popularized about this hadith being narrated with "and my sunnah" instead of "and my progeny" is only one narration. All scholars have flagged this version of this hadith because it did not emerge until after the second century AH.[12] Only those who want to stir up discord among Muslims popularize this version. Any objective person would agree that the sunnah of the Prophet would not be clear and distinct without assigning certain competent individuals who can translate that noble sunnah into daily behavior and actions—individuals who can be examples of the

Prophet's character in society so that the Prophet can be emulated by modeling them and their morals and manners. The Prophet appointed his custodians and specified their names and their count, which is the same count as the disciples of Jesus, the son of Mary: twelve successors.[13] "We made them imams, guiding by Our command, and We revealed to them the performance of good deeds, the maintenance of prayers, and the giving of zakat, and they used to worship Us" (Quran 21: 73).

The names of the twelve divinely-appointed imams are:

1. Ali son of Abu Talib (23 BH–40 AH/595–661 CE), the Prophet's cousin, his brother, and his son-in-law by means of marriage to his daughter, Fatimah al-Zahra, Leader of the Women of the Worlds (8 BH–11 AH/605–632 CE)

2. Hassan son of Ali (2–50 AH/625–670 CE)

3. Hussain son of Ali, the martyr who was massacred in Karbala, thirsty and displaced (3–61 AH/625–680 CE)

4. Ali son of Hussain (Ali al-Sajjad) (38–95 AH/659–712 CE)

5. Muhammad son of Ali (Muhammad al-Baqir) (57–

114 AH/676–733 CE)

6. Jafar son of Muhammad (Jafar al-Sadiq) (83–148 AH/702– 765 CE)

7. Musa son of Jafar (Musa al-Kadhim) (128–183 AH/745–799 CE)

8. Ali son of Musa (Ali al-Ridha) (148–203 AH/765– 818 CE)

9. Muhammad son of Ali (Muhammad al-Jawad) (195– 220 AH/811–835 CE)

10. Ali son of Muhammad (Ali al-Hadi) (212–254 AH/828–868 CE)

11. Hassan son of Ali (Hassan al-Askari) (232–260 AH/846–873 CE)

12. Muhammad son of Hassan (al-Mahdi), the Awaited One. He was born on the fifteenth of Shaban of the year 255 AH (864 CE). God hid him for a cause related to the journey of the universe and the end of the revolution of the world toward justice and equity, "They desire to put out the light of God with their mouths, but God is intent on perfecting His light though the faithless should be averse. It is He who has sent His Apostle with the guidance and the religion of truth, that He may make it prevail over all religions, though the

polytheists should be averse" (Quran 9: 32–33).

Based on this, two important issues relate to the concept of leadership (imamate) that are innate to it and to God's choosing of the twelve successors: knowledge and infallibility.

Knowledge of successors (imams)

God, the Almighty, says, "We have sent down the reminder to you so that you may clarify for the people that which has been sent down to them" (Quran 16: 44). If the Prophet must have the attributes and qualities that enable him to understand God's reminder, or message, and to communicate it to people, then his custodian and successor must have the same attributes and qualities. If not, the message would lose its effect after the Prophet's departure from this world, and its divine goal would not be accomplished. It has been repeatedly narrated about the Prophet that he said in more than one instance, "I am the city of knowledge and Ali is its gate."[14] The Commander of the Faithful, Ali son of Abu Talib, used to say, "The Prophet of God taught me a thousand chapters of knowledge, from each chapter open a thousand chapters."[15]

He and other successors (imams) from the progeny of

Prophet Muhammad are the ones these oft-repeated hadiths referred to and history spoke of, recounting their transparent conduct, the fact that they were the most knowledgeable, and that all Muslims referred to them for guidance. They did not need to ask people. However, people, even those who were hostile to them, could not help but ask them; these hostile people included rulers, leaders, and emirs. The above hadith quoting Imam Ali clearly states that he had the keys to various types of knowledge, opening their doors by God's benevolence and providence. By the same proof and logic, this is also true regarding the eleven imams following Imam Ali, who were chosen by God from among all the humans in the world.

The infallibility of successors (imams)

As reason maintains that Prophet Muhammad has employed the system of custodianship to sustain the message and supervise its execution, abiding by God's command, "Obey God and obey the Apostle and those vested with authority among you" (Quran 4:59), another attribute should be exhibited by those vested with authority. Infallibility is required to preserve the message and to introduce the exemplar that can be modeled to prevent deviation from the path of God and His prophet. It is unimaginable that, after the

Prophet, obedience be required to the commands of people who can make mistakes, omit, or forget.

Requiring obedience to people who commit sins and misdeeds is inconceivable. Therefore, reason dictates that the custodian possesses the attribute of infallibility, just as the Prophet did, to guarantee the communication of the message without disturbance in its entirety to people and to guarantee maintenance of the message. Thus, the mission is carried on by exemplars who can be models spiritually, mentally, and behaviorally.

Our Vision

Our Vision

Acquiring Moral Attributes

Individuals should acquire the attributes and qualities that God has commanded them to acquire. Simply believing in God and His existence is not enough if it is not translated into action. The word 'rabb: Arabic رب,' which translates into 'Lord' in English, also refers to an educator in Arabic. Thus, the created human can embody God's attributes, thereby becoming closer to the creator at every moment in a journey that continues until the end of life: "O man! You are laboring toward your Lord laboriously, and you will encounter Him" (Quran 84: 6). The Prophet embodied the attributes of God and was depicted in the Quran as, "And indeed you possess a great character" (Quran 68: 4), making him an example for humanity to follow. "In the Apostle of God there is certainly for you a good exemplar, for those who look forward to God and the Last Day, and remember God greatly" (Quran 33: 21).

The core and foundation of all worthy moral attributes is justice. Thus, justice has been stipulated for many matters of everyday life to spread social equality and fair practice daily. God sanctions this foundation as a requirement for many daily affairs such as serving as a witness, being the leader in congregational prayers, reciting the hadiths of the Prophet and his twelve successors, and leading society.

The requirement of justice is most crucial for jurists who issue religious edicts. It is stipulated most highly for leadership and administrative positions because these positions are the jurisdiction of prophets and successors chosen by God to carry His message. Taking over such positions without having a high degree of piety and strength would amount to tyranny.

The vision of Shia Muslims originates from this principle. Our jurists hold that the future of the universe belongs to true believers and that God's promise shall be fulfilled. The first practical step toward fulfilling this promise is for people to embody God's attributes and practice the teachings of the religion. We Shia Muslims and our jurists have paid a high price by enduring inequity and harassment to spread justice, equality, and human rights. God has provided incentives, means, and motives for humans to achieve progress and prosperity and compete to do good. He cast humans into different colors, languages,

and qualities: "Were it not for God's repelling the
people by means of one another, the earth would
surely have been corrupted; but God is gracious to the
world's creatures" (Quran 2: 251). "Mankind were a
single community; then God sent the prophets as
bearers of good news and as warners, and He sent
down with them the Book with the truth, that it may
judge between the people concerning that about
which they differed, and none differed in it except
those who had been given it, after the manifest proofs
had come to them, out of envy among themselves.
Then God guided those who had faith to the truth of
what they differed in, by His will, and God guides
whomever He wishes to a straight path" (Quran 2:
213). This guidance will be realized in its best state
when justice is established, and tyranny and injustice
are eradicated by the last of the successors, the
awaited Imam al-Mahdi.

The Age of Justice

As mentioned earlier, Shia Muslims believe, like other
Abrahamic faiths, that God's promise of an age of
justice will surely be fulfilled and the divine purpose
of the creation will be achieved: "God has promised
those of you who have faith and do righteous deeds
that He will surely make them successors in the earth

just as He made those who were before them successors, and He will surely establish for them their religion, which He has approved for them, and that He will surely change their state to security after their fear" (Quran 24: 55). This will be overseen by the last of the twelve successors to the Prophet, the awaited Imam al-Mahdi: "What remains of God's provision is better for you, should you be faithful, and I am not a keeper over you" (Quran 11: 86).

God describes this return as "the victory (of justice)": "And they say, 'When will this judgement be, should you be truthful?' Say, 'On the day of judgement their [newly found] faith shall not avail the faithless, nor will they be granted any respite.' So, turn away from them, and wait. They too are waiting" (Quran 32: 28–30). As such, this is a message of reassurance for those who may face oppression and persecution because of their faith to remain patient and avoid engagement and argument with their aggressors and antagonists, because the victory of justice is inevitable.

On that day (i.e., the day justice is restored), people will enter the true religion individually and in groups. The reason may be because, at that time, knowledge will be available and easy to attain, reason and logic will dominate, and lies and falsehood will be unmasked. God says in the Quran, "When God's help comes with victory and you see the people entering God's religion in throngs, then celebrate the praise of your Lord, and plead to Him for forgiveness. Indeed, He is all-clement" (Quran 110: 1–3). This age will see the end of arguments.

Human knowledge will reach its highest level. Logically, any other claims to truth will not be accepted.

The return of Imam al-Mahdi is depicted as a sign of God: "The day when some of your Lord's signs do come, faith shall not benefit any soul that had not believed beforehand and had not earned some goodness in its faith. Say, 'Wait! We too are waiting!'" (Quran 6: 158).

The Way Forward

The Way Forward

Based on the preceding discussion of the identity, beliefs, and vision that clearly define a path, Shia Muslims adopt a way forward.

Leadership in the Absence of Imam al-Mahdi

The legitimate authority

Based on the directives of the Prophet's successors, the twelve imams from his progeny, in the absence of Imam al-Mahdi, we Shia Muslims refer to just jurists in our temporal and spiritual matters. These jurists expend all their efforts to obtain religious rulings by extracting them from the Quran and from established, true, and validated sunnah, consensus, and reason. Thus, Shia Muslim jurists are living religious references people refer to in their worldly and otherworldly matters (e.g., prayers, fasting, pilgrimage to Mecca) and transactions such as contracts, promises, and other social matters. Some prominent jurists have stood out since the time of the greater occultation of Imam al- Mahdi, which started in 329 AH (940 CE). They have come to be called the *mujtahidin* of the community, or the great scholars. Some of the most prominent ones were the following:

- Shaykh Muhammad ibn Yaqub al-Kulayni (328 AH, 940 CE)
- Shaykh Abu Jafar Muhammad ibn Ali al-Saduq (381 AH, 992 CE)
- Shaykh Muhammad ibn al-Numan al-Akbari, also known as al-Mufid (413 AH, 1022 CE)
- Shaykh Abu Muhammad Nasir al-Din al-Tusi (460 AH, 1067 CE)
- Shaykh Muhammad Hassan al-Najafi (1266 AH, 1849 CE)
- Shaykh Murtada al-Ansari (1281 AH, 1864 CE)
- The Modernizer Mirza Hassan al-Shirazi (1312 AH, 1895 CE)
- Sayyid Muhammad Kadhim al-Yazdi (1337 AH, 1918 CE)
- Sayyid Muhsin al-Hakim (1390 AH, 1970 CE)
- Sayyid Abu al-Qasim al-Musawi al-Khoei (1413 AH, 1992 CE)

May God bless their souls.

The plurality of jurists, authorities, and fatwas

Shia Muslims have ample intellectual opportunities to seek knowledge and rise to the level where one becomes a *mufti* (Arabic: مُفتي "ruler", "Judge"). This is a journey that is never easy. On this path, one's religious authority is not recognized until one demonstrates one's knowledge to colleagues and students by means of research, teaching, writing, and improvised free debates. The centers of knowledge and research *hawzah*(Arabic: حَوزة "seminary") have always been teeming with scholars and jurists who enrich and advance knowledge. They contributed greatly to preserving and presenting Shiism despite the persecution and wrongdoings that they endured, which included defamation, falsification, imprisonment, torture, expulsion, andexecution.

The presence of numerous religious authorities leads to a plurality in legal views *fatwas* (Arabic: فتوى "verdict"), yet multiple and sometimes diverse views among jurists have certainly contributed to preserving Shiism in the face of difficult political storms on one hand and supporting knowledge and progress on the other. Any objective and, indeed, reasonable observer would not see this as negative but, on the contrary, as something that is positive. Yet with the existing plurality of legal views, the natural tendency of the believers has been to follow the rulings of the most qualified jurist (as established by the religious authorities and experts in Islamic seminaries) while simultaneously maintaining respect and reverence for all the others.

Preparation for the Age of the Return of Imam al-Mahdi

For several related reasons (and because history describes the many calamities and paradoxes that Muslims, in general, and the followers of the Prophet's progeny, in particular, have gone through), several phenomena appear in the plan for the way forward for Shias to prepare for the age of justice and equity in the absence of Imam al-Mahdi.

Prayers and supplication
A group of Shias believe that no action, movement, idea, or reform plan would be useful because the true and proper reform process falls in the domain of the infallible twelfth imam. Therefore, they settle for prayers and supplication to God to hasten his return to reinstate justice and equity. However, this idea is viewed as waiting with prudence and only passive anticipation. It does not rise to understanding the true intentions of religious practice. It has a superficial understanding of religion, reducing it to merely practicing religious rituals and ceremonies yet failing to address other dimensions of practical life in the

community (e.g., service to humanity and betterment of social conditions).

This is not a new position for Muslims or for others who believe in the idea of a savior. There have always existed believers who lacked the awareness, maturity, and intellectual foundations that could raise them to what should be truly aspired to. Moreover, this belief is contradictory to the principles of enjoining good and forbidding the reprehensible that Islamic doctrine sees as necessary to establish the religion.

Power and armed conflict

Some ancient and modern Shia Muslim scholars and intellectuals believe that the most important factor that can facilitate the return of Imam al-Mahdi is establishing a government based on Islamic legislation to prepare for the state he is expected to establish. Although these scholars made up a very small proportion of jurists throughout the ages, some movements were founded based on this idea and some of them established princedoms and governorates during the Age of Absence. Some of these include the Hamdanid state in Aleppo,[16] the Fatimids in Egypt,[17] the Buyids in Iran and Iraq,[18] the Safavids in Iran,[19] the Mazidis in Iraq and the Gulf,[20] Banu Ammar[21] and al-Hamadah[22] in northern Lebanon, and the Uyunids in the eastern part of Najd in the Arabian Peninsula.[23] It should be noted that the term 'Shia states' should be used with caution here because there is controversy about their roots, goals, and attributes. Some of these rebellions may have started with correct doctrines, practices, and foundations. Nevertheless, they failed to establish justice. For example, the injustice of the Safavids forced Shaykh Ali son of al-Hussain al-Karaki (940 AH/1534 CE) to flee Iran and settle in Najaf.

Co-existence and intellectual and spiritual growth

Many Shia Muslim scholars and jurists have an intermediate opinion that they believe will not lead to apathy and superficiality nor to a state of tension and hostility that would prevent the spread of knowledge to all people. This can be achieved by working to educate all Muslims, wherever they are, to be good citizens, to and peacefully integrate in their homelands, , and to respect the rights of others. While striving to integrate, they should also strive to adhere to their religion and noble traditions, strengthening themselves with knowledge, awareness, and ethical standards. This, in turn, will allow them to be respectable heralds and missionaries and contribute to establishing a broad, diverse culture that can build a global movement based on the rule of justice. This is important given that most religions and sects believe in the inevitable emergence of a global savior to spread justice and equity and eradicate injustice and oppression.

The importance of coexistence becomes more evident when considering that Muslims believe that Jesus will descend to Earth and most People of the Book[24] will follow him. God says in the Quran, "Though they did not kill him, nor did they crucify him, but so it was made to appear to them. Indeed, those who differ concerning him are surely in doubt about him: they do not have any knowledge of that beyond following conjectures, and certainly they did not kill him. Rather, God raised him up toward Himself, and God is all-mighty, all-wise. There is none among the People of the Book but will surely believe in him before his death; and on the Day of Resurrection he will be a witness against them" (Quran 4: 157–159).

Prophet Jesus will join Imam al-Mahdi in his divine mission. The scholars and spiritual adherents of the People of the Book, through their humility, will find that the doctrine of Imam al-Mahdi is one based on love and charity: "And surely you will find the nearest of them in affection to the faithful to be those who say 'We are Christians.' That is because there are priests and monks among them, and because they are not arrogant" (Quran 5: 82).

At that time, the divine goal of uniting humanity will be achieved and people, by reason, wisdom, and logic, will believe in and enter the one religion of God in large groups: "When God's help comes with victory and you see the people entering God's religion in throngs, then celebrate the praise of your Lord, and plead to Him for forgiveness. Indeed, He is all-clement" (Quran 110: 1–3). The Quran indicates that religion can never be implemented using force but by using reason and explaining the difference between right and wrong: "There is no compulsion in religion: rectitude has become distinct from error" (Quran 2: 256). Imposing beliefs on individual people by force is inconceivable, never mind forcing large groups of people into a certain religion.

The Duties of Shia Muslims Today

Based on the preceding definitions of our identity, our vision, and the way forward, our just jurists, who have all the qualifications to issue fatwas and have the standing to represent Imam al-Mahdi, assert and advise Muslims in general, and the faithful believers in particular, that their role at this time is to be good citizens and integrate into their societies and homelands while preserving their religious identity and noble traditions according to the following principles.

PROTECTING OURSELVES: Since we are individuals who believe in the right to live, we should uphold this right and use it to protect ourselves while abiding by the laws of the land we live in.

PROTECTING OUR INTERESTS: Since we are a community that has unique interests, our interests should be protected and recognized by others.

PROTECTING OUR SOCIAL ROLE: The principle of equality dictates that we should play a role in shaping the societies we live in. The faith and beliefs we have are rich with ideas and principles that propel us to build and develop any society we live in.

PROTECTING THE RIGHT TO COEXIST: Our community today is global, diverse, rich, and comes from various backgrounds. This requires us to coexist with others while preserving our identity, thereby allowing every community its own distinct features.

Believers should take this as sound advice that is full of wisdom and insight. It is a guideline that places the responsibility on all faithful believers, wherever they are, to expend their efforts to attain cooperation and harmony, to implement this advice based on the principle that humankind is the vicegerent of God on Earth, and to enrich the Earth with justice and equity. After this divine endowment and prudent legislative advice, the process of change and progress is in the hands of the faithful themselves, particularly the ones who take the lead in society such as religious, social, intellectual, economic, and political leaders. God, the Almighty, says, "Indeed God does not change a people's lot, unless they change what is in their souls" (Quran 13: 11).

We ask the Almighty to make this presentation useful and beneficial in illuminating the path, defining milestones, uniting hearts, and explaining the truth to anyone who seeks it. We ask the Almighty to make it a contribution toward spreading knowledge, security, stability, and peace among humankind and toward living a gracious life and achieving a better future.

Appendix 1

Names of the Fourteen Infallibles

This is a list of those whom we Shia Muslims believe to be the infallible people who God designated for us to emulate. The list includes fourteen people including Prophet Muhammad, his daughter Lady Fatimah, and his twelve successors.

title | full name | also known as | date of birth | place of birth | date of death | place of burial

1. Prophet | Muhammad son of Abdullah | Muhammad al-Mustafa | 53 BH (570 CE) | Mecca, Arabia | 11 AH (632 CE) | Medina, Arabia

2. Lady | Fatimah daughter of Muhammad | Fatimah al-Zahra | 8 BH (615 CE) | Medina, Arabia | 11 AH (632 CE) | Medina, Arabia

3. Imam | Ali son of Abu Talib | Ali al-Murtadha | 23 BH (959 CE) | Mecca, Arabia | 40 AH (661 CE) | Najaf, Iraq

4. Imam | Hassan son of Ali | al-Hassan al-Mujtaba | 2 AH (624 CE) | Medina, Arabia | 50 AH (670 CE) | Medina, Arabia

5. Imam | Hussain son of Ali | al-Hussain al-Shaheed | 3 AH (626 CE) | Medina, Arabia | 61 AH (680 CE) | Karbala, Iraq

6. Imam | Ali son of Hussain | Ali al-Sajjad | 38 AH (659 CE) | Medina, Arabia | 95 AH (713 CE) | Medina, Arabia

7. Imam | Muhammad son of Ali | Muhammad al-Baqir | 57 AH (767 CE) | Medina, Arabia | 114 AH (733 CE) | Medina, Arabia

8. Imam | Jafar son of Muhammad | Jafar al-Sadiq | 83 AH (702 CE) | Medina, Arabia | 148 AH (765 CE) | Medina, Arabia

9. Imam | Musa son of Jafar | Musa al-Kadhim | 128 AH (745 CE) | Medina, Arabia | 183 AH (791 CE) | Baghdad, Iraq

10. Imam | Ali son of Musa | Ali al-Ridha | 148 AH (765 CE) | Medina, Arabia | 203 AH (818 CE) | Mashhad, Iran

11. Imam | Muhammad son of Ali | Muhammad al-Jawad | 195 AH (811 CE) | Medina, Arabia | 220

AH (835 CE) | Baghdad, Iraq

12. Imam | Ali son of Muhammad | Ali al-Hadi | 212 AH (827 CE) | Medina, Arabia | 254 AH (868 CE) | Samarra, Iraq

13. Imam | Hassan son of Ali | Hassan al-Askari | 232 AH (846 CE) | Medina, Arabia | 260 AH (874 CE) | Samarra, Iraq

14. Imam | Muhammad son of Hassan | al-Hujjah, al-Mahdi, al-Muntadhar | 255 AH (869 AD) | Samarra, Iraq | still alive

Images of the Shrines of the Infallibles

The following are images of the holy shrines of these infallible people.[25]

1. Al-Nabi Mosque and shrine where the Holy Prophet Muhammad son of Abdullah and his daughter Lady Fatimah (p) are buried. Medina, Arabian Peninsula.

2. The shrine of Imam Ali son of Abu Talib. Najaf, Iraq.

3. Al-Baqi Cemetery before demolition.

4. After demolition: The demolished shrines of Imams Hassan son of Ali, Ali son of Hussain (al-Sajjad), Muhammad son of Ali (al-Baqir), and Jafar son of Muhammad (al-Sadiq), al-Baqi Cemetery. Medina, Arabian Peninsula. Twice the extreme Wahhabi group has demolished these shrines; the first time was 1805 CE (1220 AH), and after rebuilding it the second time was on April 21, 1926 CE (Shawwal 8, 1344 AH). It remains as shown here.

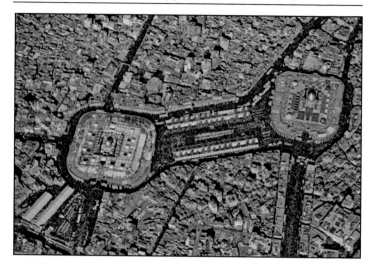

5. Satellite view of the shrines of Imam Hussain son of Ali and his brother Abbas. Karbala, Iraq.

6. Night view of the area between the shrines of Imam Hussain and his brother Abbas.

7. Imam Hussain's shrine.

8. A piece of earth from Imam Hussain's grave. It
changes to blood every year in the middle of the tenth
day of Muharram (the day he was martyred and the first

month of the Islamic calendar).

9. Aerial image of the annual pilgrimage of visitors to
Imam Hussain's shrine (Arbaeen), which occurs on the
twentieth of Safar (the second month of the Islamic
calendar). Every year more than twenty million
visitors come walking from a hundred miles away to
visit this holy shrine to show respect and commitment
to Imam Hussain for his stand for justice and dignity.

10. Another image of the Arbaeen pilgrimage next to the shrine.

11. The shrine of Imams Musa al-Kadhim and Muhammad al-Jawad. Kadhmiyyah, Baghdad, Iraq.

12. The shrine of Imam Ali al-Ridha. Mashhad, Iran.

13. The shrine of Imams Ali al-Hadi and Hassan al-Askari, Samarra, Iraq.

1. That holy shrine after an attack by an extreme
    Wahhabi group on February 22, 2006.

15. Remodeling of the shrine.

Appendix 2

The Leading Shia Muslim Jurists During the Past One Thousand Years

From the martyrdom of the eleventh infallible imam, Hassan al-Askari, on the eighth of Rabi al-Awwal 260 AH (874 CE) and the time that his son, the twelfth infallible imam, Imam al-Mahdi, went into occultation until today, Shia seminaries have produced hundreds of qualified jurists, most of whom assumed leadership in Shia Muslim communities around the world. About two hundred of them were in the highest positions of worldwide religious leadership. We include the minimum list of names that should be known to everyone—those who have been the leading Shia religious jurists worldwide in their times for the past one thousand years or so. These names are just a sampling, and we could add more to the list.

title | full name | also known as | place of residence | death AH | death CE

Shaykh | Muhammad ibn Yaqub | al-Kulayni | Qom, Iran | 329 | 941

Shaykh | Muhammad ibn Ali ibn Hussain | al-Saduq | Baghdad, Iraq | 381 | 991

Shaykh | Muhammad ibn Muhammad ibn Numaan | al-Mufid | Baghdad, Iraq | 413 | 1022

Sayyid | Ali ibn Hussain | al-Murtada | Baghdad, Iraq | 436 | 1044

Shaykh | Muhammad ibn Hassan | al-Tusi | Baghdad and Najaf, Iraq | 460 | 1067

Shaykh | Jafar ibn Hassan | al-Hilli | Hillah, Iraq | 676 | 1277

Shaykh | Jamal al-Din Hassan ibn Yusuf ibn al-Mutahhar
| al-Hilli | Hillah, Iraq | 726 | 1325

Shaykh | Muhammad ibn Jamal al-Din ibn Makki | al-Shahid al-Awwal | Hillah, Iraq | 786 | 1384

Shaykh | Zayn al-Din ibn Ali | al-Shahid al-Thaani | Jebaa, Lebanon | 965 | 1558

Shaykh | Jafar ibn Khider | Kashif al-Ghitaa | Najaf, Iraq | 1228 | 1813

Shaykh | Murtada ibn Muhammad | al-Ansari | Najaf, Iraq | 1281 | 1864

Sayyid | Muhammad Hassan | al-Shirazi | Samarra, Iraq | 1312 | 1894

Shaykh | Muhammad Kadhim ibn Hussain al-Harati | al-Akhond | Najaf, Iraq | 1329 | 1911

Shaykh | Abid al-Karim | al-Hairi al-Yazdi | Qom, Iran | 1355 | 1937 Shaykh | Muhammad Hussain | al-Naiyni | Najaf, Iraq | 1355 | 1936

Sayyid | Abu al-Hassan | al-Asfahaani | Samarra and Najaf, Iraq | 1365 | 1945

Shaykh | Muhammad Hussain | Kashif al-Ghitaa | Najaf, Iraq | 1373 | 1953

Sayyid | Hussain | al-Burujirdi | Qom, Iran | 1380 | 1960

Sayyid | Abd al-Hadi al-Hussaini | al-Shirazi | Samarra and Najaf, Iraq | 1382 | 1962

Sayyid | Muhsin al-Tabatabai | al-Hakim | Najaf, Iraq | 1390 | 1970 Sayyid | Abu al-Qasim al-Musawi | al-Khoei | Najaf, Iraq | 1413 | 1992

Sayyid | Muhammad Rida al-Musawi | al-Ghulpayghani | Qom, Iran | 1414 | 1993

A traditional study circle at Najaf seminary.

Shaykh Muhammad al-Numan al-Akbari al- Mufid, the first highest authorized jurist after Imam al-Mahdi.

Shaykh Muhammad ibn Hassan al-Tusi, the first highest jurist who moved from Baghdad and established the Najaf seminary.

Shaykh Murtada al- Ansari, the most creative intellectual. He made a major transition in the principles of jurisprudence in seminarian history, and his books are still at the top of the highest-level studies in seminaries.

Sayyid Muhsin al-Tabatabai al-Hakim, one of the highest Shia jurists who had the largest number of worldwide Shia followers.

Sayyid Abu al-Qasim al-Khoei, the most famous high jurist who educated and graduated over one hundred jurists from his school.

Sayyid Ali al-Husseini al-Sistani, currently the highest Shia jurist worldwide. He is the first Shia jurist in history to visit the United Nations General Secretary to thank him for his role in bringing peace in the Middle East.

Shaykh Hussain Wahid Khorasani, one of the highest jurists and educators in the Qom seminary.

The Leading Shia Muslim Speakers During the Past Few Decades

Shaykh Muhammad Taqi Falsafai, Iran, 1908–1998.

Shaykh Ahmad al-Waeli, Iraq, 1928–2003.

Moulana Mirza
Mohammed Athar,
India, 1937–2016.

Shaykh Talib Jauhari,
Pakistan, 1939–.

Sayyid Monir al- Khabaz,
Al-Qatif, Arabian
Peninsula, 1964–.

Notes

1. The verses of the Holy Quran are from the translation by Ali Quli Qarai with minor edits where needed.

2. Twelver refers to the school of thought that believes in twelve infallible successors who are responsible for handling the message of Islam and leading the Muslim nation after the death of Prophet Muhammad (pbuh&hp).

3. consensus - *ijmaa* (Arabic: إجماع). For certain conditions/cases, there is neither an apparent verse from the Quran nor clearly delineating narrations from infallibles available to establish a verdict (Islamic rule). For some of these conditions/cases, all the companions of the infallibles or all the great religious authorities during their time and after, had the same opinion of the Islamic rule concerning a given condition/case. Thus, this indicates with near certainty that those companions and great religious authorities must have acquired that opinion or view from the teachings of an infallible and provides sufficient confidence that there is a valid edict that an

infallible issued but which we may have missed. This is called *ijmaa*. *Ijmaa* is an Arabic word meaning all agree on something.

4. Mutazilah (Arabic: المعتزلة) is a group of Sunni Muslims who adopted a different way the from the Ashaa'irah (Arabic: الأشاعرة) group in dealing with Islamic rulings. Mutazilah share similar beliefs with Shia Muslims in that they concede that the mind is the principal tool to understand oneness, and to understand the Quran and hadith (after clarification and making sure which hadiths are true and which ones are not).

5. The *sunnah* (Arabic: سنة) of the Prophet is what has been established by the Prophet as a saying, act, or endorsement. This includes endorsing a saying or an act by staying silent, thereby signaling his satisfaction and lack of disapproval, because he is obligated to enjoin good and forbid evil, which requires that he interfere to terminate corruption and anything that violates the divine message. *Sunnah* is a doctrinal term that has nothing to do with classifying Muslims as Sunnis and non-Sunnis. That classification has political dimensions and was not devised until after the departure of the Prophet from this world. The contemporary term *Sunni* refers to various doctrinal

and jurisprudential sects such as the Hanafis (Arabic: الحنفي), Malikis (Arabic: المالكي), Shafiis (Arabic: الشافعي), and Hanbalis (Arabic: الحنبلي). Chapter 110 of the Quran: "When God's help comes with victory, and you see the people entering God's religion in throngs, then celebrate the praise of your Lord, and plead to Him for forgiveness. Indeed, He is all-clement."

6. This refers to the part of the verse that says, "Today I have perfected your religion for you, and I have completed my blessing upon you, and I have approved Islam as your religion" (Quran 5:3).

7. Ghadir Khumm is a place in the Arabian Peninsula between the two holy cities: Mecca and Medina. Ghadir means a small river or pond. It is the place that over 120,000 pilgrims witnessed the Prophet (pbuh&hp) officially stating that Ali son of Abu Talib (p) was to be the first successor after him.

8. Dhu al-Hijjah is the name of the twelfth month of the Islamic calendar. The twelve Islamic months are as follows:

1. Muharram
2. Safar
3. Rabi al-Awwal
4. Rabi al-Thani

5. Jamadi al-Awwal

6. Jamadi al-Thani

7. Rajab

8. Shaban

9. Ramadan

10. Shawwal

11. Dhu al-Qadah

12. Dhu al-Hijjah

9. Muhajirun (Arabic: المهاجرون The Emigrants) were a group of people who accepted Islam in Mecca then emigrated to Medina right after the Prophet (pbuh&hp).

10. Ansar (Arabic: الأنصار "The Helpers", "supporters", "defenders", "upholders", "advocates") are the inhabitants of Medina who welcomed and took the Prophet Muhammad and his followers into their homes when they emigrated from Mecca.

11. Examiners have affirmed that this hadith is weak and there are unknown people in its chain of narrators. Its first narrator is Malik ibn Anas (94–179 AH) in his book *Al-muwatta* (2:899). He did not live in the early stage of Islam.

12. The hadith of the twelve imams—"All the imams are from Quraysh"—is one of the oft-repeated hadiths

that are narrated by all hadith collections of all Islamic sects and divisions.

13. Shaykh Muhammad Ridha al-Mudhaffar, *The True Guidance to the Righteous Path*, 2:332.

14. This is one of the recurrent hadiths narrated by all Muslims. Al-Muttaqi al-Hindi has narrated it in *Muntakhab kanz al-ummal* on the margin of *Musnad Ahmad* quoting Ali and Jabir al-Ansari (5:30).

15. The Hamdanid (Arabic: الحمدانية) state (276–394 AH/890 –1004 CE) appeared because of the conflict between the Abbasids and the Turks. It was founded by Hamdan son of Hamdun who was known for his allegiance to the Prophet's progeny, thus the name Hamdanids. His lineage traces to Banu Taghlib, a branch of Banu Rabiah. Based in Mosul, he gained control of some parts of Iraq and the Levant. Later, the Hamdanids moved their capital to Aleppo. There were several wars between them and the Byzantines in which their leader Saif al-Dawlah al-Hamdani had famous heroic feats. The Hamdanid state ended after the death of Saif al-Dawlah and the rising clashes among the Hamdanids which enabled the Fatimids to seize Aleppo and end the Hamdanid rule.

16. The Fatimid (Arabic: الفاطميون) state (296–566

AH/909 –1171 CE) was founded because of the Abbasids and their outrageous oppression of the followers of the Prophet's progeny that made them flee to North Africa and the Arabian Maghreb. They began their political movement and rebellion against the Abbasid Caliphate from a region in Africa they called al-Mahdiah. They advanced until they conquered Egypt and took it under their control, founding al-Azhar University. They expanded their reach to vast areas including some of the Levant and Hijaz to the east and most of Africa to the west. Their state receded because they lost their justness and began oppressing their people, which weakened them gradually, enabling Saladin to conquer the Levant and then Egypt easily.

17. The Buyid (Arabic: البويهيون) state (320–447 AH/932–1055 CE) was founded by Abu Shuja Buya and his three sons in Kerman and Isfahan in Iran. It then expanded to rule Iran and control the Abbasid Caliphate without overthrowing or isolating it.

18. The Safavid (Arabic: الصفويون) state (906–1148 AH/1500–1735 CE) was founded by Sunni Sufis in Tabriz under the command of Shah Ismail. After gaining control of Iran, the Safavids officially declared themselves as Shias. They entered many wars against

the Ottomans for the control of Iraq.

19. Banu Mazidi (Arabic: المزيديون / بنو مزيد) were from Iraq and traced their lineage to Banu Asad. Their state was founded by Ali Abu al-Hasan son of Mazid al-Asadi in 388 AH/998 CE in a town called al-Nil near the city of Hillah on the west bank of the Euphrates river between Kufa and Baghdad.

20. Banu Ammar (Arabic: بنو عمّار) was one of the Arabian Maghreb's Berber tribes. They became Shia during the rule of the Fatimids. They traced their lineage to Abu Muhammad al-Hassan son of Ammar, who became famous during the rule of the Fatimid Caliph al-Aziz Billah. They later settled down in Tripoli where the Fatimids appointed al- Hassan son of Ammar as the judge in 457 AH (1065 CE).

He paid allegiance to the Fatimids until 462 AH (1070 CE) when he declared independence. Banu Ammar expanded their reach to Antakya to the north and the vicinity of Beirut to the south. Historians state that architecture, the economy, and sciences boomed during their rule. Their state was overthrown in 502 AH (1109 CE) because of the Crusades in a siege that continued for more than seven years.

21. Al-Hamadah (Arabic: آل حمادة) ruled Tripoli for

approximately two hundred years beginning in 1060 AH (1650 CE). They went through strenuous times because of the ongoing clashes between the Safavids and the Ottomans to a degree that some historians believe that they declared their conversion to the Sunni sect.

22. The Uyunids (Arabic: العَيونية) ruled for approximately two hundred years beginning in 460 AH (1067 CE). One of their most prominent leaders was Prince Abd Gud son of Ali al-Uyuni al-Ahsai al-Ibrahim. They resisted the attacks of the Qarmatians for years during which many of them were killed and their bodies burned.

23. 'People of the Book' is an Islamic term that refers to followers of the religions with an actual book from God, such as Jews, and Christians, also known as followers of the great monotheistic religions.

24. The images have been taken from the official sites of the shrines of the infallible imams, especially al-Atabah al-Hussainiyah and al-Atabah al-Abbasiyah.

About the Author

Sayyid Mohammad Baqir Kashmiri, the son of His Eminence Sayyid Ali Naqi and the grandson of Ayatullah Sayyid Murtadha al-Ridhawi al-Kashmiri, comes from a renowned family recognized for their high levels of education, piety, and dedicated service in supporting the Muslim community. The Kashmiri family links to the family of Prophet Muhammad (pbuh&hp) through the lineage of Musa al-Mubarqa', son of Imam Muhammad al-Jawad (p). The family became known socially by the last name of "Kashmiri" because their grandfather lived in Kashmir for a time as a preacher and resident religious scholar.

With religious service in Iraq, Iran, Pakistan, and India for nearly a thousand years, the Kashmiri family has established a reputation of integrity and honor, depicted by the family's love of acquiring knowledge and their passion to serve the community in which they live. As such, Sayyid Mohammad Baqir Kashmiri completed most of his religious studies in Iran, beginning in the Holy City of Mashhad and later continuing in the Holy City of Qom. Sayyid studied under the guidance of the most prominent teachers in the Muslim world such as Shaykh Ibrahim Sibawayh, Sayyid Sahib Mashallah, Shaykh Muhammad Ridha al-Sadiq, Shaykh Muhammad Taqi al-Gharawi, Sayyid Jawad Shubbar, Ayatullah Shaykh Hassan al-Jawahiri, Ayatullah Shaykh Naser Makarem Shirazi, Ayatullah Sayyid Kamal al-Haydari, and Ayatullah Sayyid Muhammad Ridha al-Husseini al-Jalali.

Sayyid Kashmiri represents ten late and living jurists in Qom and Najaf seminaries. He received a wikala (representative proxy) from His Eminence Ayatullah Sayyid Ali al-Husseini al-Sistani to deal with all matters pertaining to the jurist in North America. As the representative of the supreme religious authority, Sayyid al-Sistani, Sayyid Kashmiri moved to Los Angeles, California, in the year 2000 where he later founded the Imam Mahdi Association of Marjaeya (I.M.A.M.), an organization intended to support the Shia community in North America by being the central point of communication between Shia Muslims in North America and their spiritual religious leadership (marjaeya) in all matters pertaining to beliefs and religious duties. Later, he and his family relocated the I.M.A.M. headquarters to Dearborn, Michigan.

As the Chairman and Religious Affairs Director of I.M.A.M, Sayyid is the primary person responsible for overseeing and coordinating all activities that require the endorsement of or adoption by a religious authority such as religious verdicts, education, and dues in North America. He is actively working to organize matters of Shia Muslims in North America in relevant areas such as worship, marriage, divorce, wills, inheritance, and other religious legal matters while adhering to the laws of the land. In addition, he often travels to different states to develop connections between various Islamic centers and to foster unity through networking.

As a writer, author, and lecturer, Sayyid Kashmiri has participated in numerous activities and projects throughout the years: he has supervised and published several Islamic magazines including *Rasikhoon*, *Reflections*, and *Fiqhona*; he has authored pieces of his own such as "Jurisprudence Manual for Youth," and he has established credibility for numerous religious authors by writing forewords for books such as *God's Emissaries*, *Islam and Christianity - Brothers at Odds*, *A Code of Practice for Muslims in the West*, *Fasting: A Haven from Hellfire*, and *Amicable Companionship*. He has given numerous speeches and written research papers and articles on various subjects including history, Quran interpretation, Islamic principles, religion, and secularism, which have resulted in "The Washington Declaration: A Code of Honor for Sunni and Shia in North America against Violence and Extremism" as well as the development of "The Roadmap for the Advancement of Shia Muslims in North America."

Sayyid continues to be active in public speaking during the month of Ramadhan, in the first ten days of Muharram, and at Islamic conferences. He teaches Islamic jurisprudence and is involved in preparing aspiring scholars to commence their religious studies at Shia seminaries. His years of service are based around his unwavering belief in the ability to develop a strong, cohesive Shia Muslim presence and community, and it is for this reason that he is continually consulted about the details of the North American community by many scholars and researchers at Islamic seminaries.

Sayyid Kashmiri is currently serving from northern Virginia in the newest I.M.A.M. location where he, his spouse, and four children have relocated to lead I.M.A.M.'s core functions.

Made in the USA
Monee, IL
12 January 2022

88332559R00059